"There are very few people in the world that have the gift of connecting to your soul through their words, and Jackie is one of those people. She unapologetically articulates the emotional spectrum of motherhood with beauty, raw honesty, and inspiration. I felt immensely connected to the truths Jackie tells in her poetry, because so many of us as mothers have been there. Thank you, Jackie, for sharing your gifts with the world and for making mothers everywhere feel less alone."

~ Jennifer Douglas, Writer, Goldfish and Chicken Nuggets

Eating Her Young: Poems for the Disruption of Motherhood

ISBN 978-1-7778484-0-8

First print edition Fall 2021

empowermentforresilience.com
jackie@empowermentforresilience.com

Book design by Stephen D. Gibson https://kingtigerbooks.com/
stephen.d.gibson@gmail.com

Eating Her Young

Poems for the Disruption of Motherhood

Dedication

For my husband Tyler and my mother Sharon – the two people who truly got me through the long days and the terrifying nights and the fear of my own oblivion. Thank you for holding my head above water when I couldn't and thank you for always believing in me and supporting me without hesitation. For all of the women who suffer from pre- and post-partum mood issues and especially for those who do not make it because the pain gets too great. May those of us who made it through speak our truths if we can so that no one suffers alone or in shame.

For Stephen who helped this book come to life, for your support, and for having the patience for details that I do not – all of my gratitude and appreciation.

And for Aya, my daughter, whose life truly has changed mine in ways that are both incalculable and tangible, and whose presence on this earth reminds me that miracles do happen and are embodied in the most beautiful and spectacular and unsuspecting ways.

CONTENTS

Prologue

I never thought that I'd be a mother. Not because I didn't meticulously plan my pregnancy or barrel headfirst into motherhood as an adventure, but because it wasn't my raison d'etre. Motherhood was not my goal. Similarly, marriage had not been a goal in my life until I met the man I would marry. And without this man, I would not be a mother, because he makes me feel like anything is possible in this life and, with him, it is. Often, people think, because of the ways I talk about motherhood, that I had an unplanned pregnancy. They think this because they think that anyone who wanted a baby, a child, would never speak about motherhood so openly, to negatively, so truthfully. Let that sink in: The only way that people can conceive of a woman telling the truth about motherhood is if they didn't mean to be a mother and they had to live with the, I guess, resentful reality of motherhood.

I may not have pined to be a mother, but I prepared to be one. I prepared in the ways one who has spent her life researching instead of really doing does: By reading all the books. I was, you see, prepared for a child while pregnant. I had read all the books. I had done all the yoga. I had been to the prenatal classes where shit got real when one of the midwives performed simulated active labour so that we would know what to look out for when it was really time to deliver. If you had tested me on my knowledge of what could happen, what might happen, what to be prepared for, what to watch out for – all in all, how to be the "perfect" pregnant pre-Mommy human, I would have aced the test. I just didn't see the reality of what came after coming.

When she came into this world, it was nothing like I had expected. Nothing like I had planned. I had a traumatic birth and honestly, many of us have. Traumatic births are hard to put your finger on and my story is not one that I want to tell in this moment, but a traumatic birth sets you up for the loss of control that you continue to experience as a woman who has become a mother overnight. One day you are one, the next day, you are multiplied and there is no going back.

This living thing that you have been planning for 40 weeks wriggles on your chest, people help you stick your breast into her mouth, she is a stranger, and she is yours forever.

I wrote the poems you are about to read during my long march, sometimes crawl, out of postpartum depression and anxiety. These poems constitute my truth of the experience of motherhood as a woman who was hit by the truck of birth, postpartum hormones, difficulty breastfeeding, and loss of identity. I am no longer afraid of that time in my life, but my memory of it sits like a stomach-ache in the same place that I created and held her body for all those months. These poems helped me to rebuild my life. They helped me to remember who I was and who I am. They helped me construct an identity of mother that slowly but surely melded with who I had always known myself to be. These poems are the patchwork of myself being pieced back together through exhaustion and terror, through hopelessness and hope, through sadness and guilt, and through the reconstruction of myself from monster to mother.

If nothing else, this book is an offering. A beacon of what I can now see as hope. Things have gotten better. So much better. And that is all I really needed to know during that time, that things can and would get better. With help and support and an outlet and medication and counseling, I am better. You can be too. Please don't give up on yourself or the life of your dreams because things got out of control or because you didn't think that joy would ever be possible again. May these poems help knit your heart and head back together again because you, you Mama, are the most important thing there is in this world. You are everything.

Memories

Old Dreams

It's okay to be sad.
Bone-tired.
Hopeless.
It's okay
Not to fit.
Feel uncomfortable.
Make space for
Yourself.
It's okay to dream
Even while
Old dreams
Crumble around you.

Mistress of the Universe

I want to give up,
But I haven't.
I want to save the world,
But I'm tired.
I want to remember who I was,
But I can't.
I want to tell my truth,
So I did.
I want to breathe freely.
I want to be in the world
Unencumbered.
I want to find ways to pray
That connect me to pure light
And freedom.
I want to not suffer.
I want to be perfect.
I want to be free of pain.
I want to taste bravery.
I want to free everyone
Of fear.
I want to try my best
And have it be enough.

I want to love and be loved.

I want my anger

To burn up.

I want autonomy.

I want a fresh start.

I want to wonder and adventure.

I want surprise

And awe.

I want to know the world.

I want to walk in sand.

I want to know pleasure.

I want to be the Mistress of My Universe.

I want to learn new things.

I want to share my gifts.

I want to know that everything will be okay.

I want everything to be okay.

Expansion

So you are scared
And sad
And lonely.
Your breaths
Are shallow
And timid,
Shrunken,
Like you don't want
To take up too much
Space.
Like breathing
Would belie
Your agony.
And the very fact
That you feel
At all.
You know the
only answer
Is to expand
But expansion
Is a risk
And risks

Always eviscerate you
Before they
Save your
Soul.

Perfection

There are all kinds of ways
Things will never be perfect.
And every way that life
Could be different.
And you stick to bland
Sameness
Like a bastion of sanity.
Normalcy.
Crushing happiness like
Insignificance.
Wondering
When that's
All the truth
You'll ever need.

Pieces of You

In this life,
There are reasons to lose
Hope
Faith
Pieces of yourself.
There are tiny
Fractures
In all of us.
Sometimes stretched
To their limit.
There are losses that feel permanent
And some that leave
Scars on the fabric of our
Souls.
There are gruesome pieces
That we try to reject
Not knowing
That the sum of those parts
Is necessary for the whole.

Glow

You will survive
This moment
Even as it threatens
To eat you
Alive.
You will be rewarded
With all the gentleness
Your heart
Desires.
Struggle is necessary
And your path
Will be laden
With snakes.
But you will rise
Darkness
Lifted from you
Like a heavy veil.
You will see
The sun again,
My Love,
And it will make you glow.

The Same Difference

Oh, but aren't you
Exquisite
In your exhaustion.
The kind
You reserve
For those you love
With a rawness
That you can't taste.
And don't you wish
That everything
Could be the same
And different
As you walk in shoes
That are too big
For you
And make you stumble
Over and over again
To your
Bloody knees

Pretty Pictures

I am so tired.
You are so tired.
We made magic.
We imprinted memories.
We ate too much.
We kept our shit together.
Mostly.
We stayed up late
Creating haphazard
Picturesque scenes
That we hope will wrap
Our children in the warmth of our love
Forever.
We hugged and kissed
And prayed.
Maybe we even cried.
We cradled our children
However they needed to be held
And we pushed through
Even when we didn't want to.

A Prayer for the New Year

I am enough.
I am worthy.
I love with all of me.
I try my very best.
I am loved.
Broken pieces
Of me
Heal over time
And with help.
I am no one's fool.
I am a woman
That I can be proud of.
I'm trying.
I will always try.
I will keep going.
By not mistaking
The stones
For the mountain.

Reborn

Sometimes
You need to lay things
Down.
Heavy burdens
Like who you thought
You were.
You have to swallow
And gasp
For air
Like a wounded
Fish
On a rock
Waiting to be
Reborn
As something
With wings.

Pears in Pieces

Sometimes
Love smells
Like sweat
And feels like
Electricity.
Sometimes love
Is failure
And feeble
Attempts at being
Something other.
Sometimes love
Is his profile
In a funny
Little
Sportscar.
Sometimes love is pears
In pieces
And middle of the night
Tears.

Dark Mind

Sometimes newborns
Make your
Skin crawl
And all of the hair
On your body
Stand at attention
In the same way that it did
When you couldn't close
Your eyes
At night
Or keep them open
Because it was a puzzle
To figure out
If you feared the darkness
Inside your mind
More then
The baby screaming
On your belly.

Birthing Under the Moon

I am
Unearthed
And sent
A flight
When I see pictures
Of soon-to-be
Mothers
Birthing under
The moon.
I am made oddly
Calm
And terrified
That a piece of me
Would,
After everything,
Trade places
With them
For another opportunity
To make it right.

Sticky Shoes

Sometimes life
Is an exquisite dance
Messy
And unpredictable
Sticky shoes
On beer-stained floors
And your face
Your face
Loving me already
Like I matter
And I do.
I really do.

Kisses

If living
In opposition
To oneself
And the world
Was truly what
Brought peace
Our bodies wouldn't
Ache for others
And our lips
Wouldn't feel
Raw
From the claw of our
Teeth
Along them
As though
Memorializing
Long dead
Kisses.

Boy Scout

I bled
On someone
Once.
Someone I thought
I loved.
But I didn't love him.
I only loved him
For saving me.
This boy scout.
This almost-man.
Once he was an
Angel
That separated me
From life
And death.
But he couldn't
Save me
From growing up
And realizing
That some men
Are never
Going to be
Enough.

Butterfly Wings

Once I was kissed
By butterfly wings
And they tasted like
Hope
And secrecy.
Once I thought
That options
Were endless
And that life was some kind
Of oyster
Pregnant
With a hidden
Pearl.
Once I sat
In a foggy car
Groping at dreams
And touching
Softness
With my lips.

Happiness

Were you ever
Happy
She asked
Not so innocently
And I gasped
And thought
Fuck yeah
How dare you
(Maybe in reverse order)
And she made me doubt
The time
Along the winding
Mountain roads
When just being
Was enough
Along with a loose
Plan
And love firmly
Unwaveringly
By my side.

Soft Lips

I once knew
A girl,
A friend really,
Who couldn't be happy
For who I was.
She was fun
And smart
And creative
And she had big soft
Lips
That I would sometimes
Kiss
But she hated the world
And herself
More than she could
Ever love
Me.

Tender Tinder

Sometimes a wildfire
Is waiting for you
In places
That you least expect.
Tender tinder
Waiting to ignite
From the lipstick-stained
Cigarette
That you carelessly
Dropped from you lips.
You think you are
Everything
And they tell you that
You are nothing
And you believe them
Because they love you
Right?

Sharp Corners

I guess
You could say
That I used to get
Embarrassed
About the stuff that
I was
But wasn't
Supposed
To be.
I guess
You could say
That I hid
Around
The sharp corners
Of my own
Peripheral
Vision
Until I allowed
Myself
To come
Fully
Into view.

Save Yourself

I won't grind myself up
And make myself into palatable perfection.
I won't spill my blood to save you
From yourself.
I will watch you
Fall.
You are not as smart
As you think you are.
Nor as courageous
As I'd like.
You don't diminish anyone
In the shadow
Of your contrived pain.
I'd like to tell you
To fuck yourself
But you're too busy
Scrambling on your knees
For forgiveness
That you will never get
And love
That you won't ever know.

Fawn

When I'm twisted up
And broken
Aimless
And fearful
Like a fawn
Left by her mother
In the long grass
I know that you are there.
I know that you will steady the ship,
Keep me on course,
Even when I want to jump into icy waters.
Even when I know I'm drowning.
You rescued me from a life of boredom
And my own betrayal of who I really am
Because you saw me.
From the first time we met,
You looked at me like I mattered
Like I mattered more than everyone,
More than anyone.
And when you wink at me across a room,
I melt.
I know that I am seen.

I know that you would hold my head

Above the water

Even if we were both going under.

There are few people in this life

Who will walk with you.

Through sadness and pain.

Through insecurity and tumult.

Through disaster-filled joy.

You walk with me even when I don't want to walk

anymore.

You drag me through the mire.

You have the biggest piece of my heart

Because you expanded it when you chose

To love me.

My heart is yours forever

Because a life where I am not walking beside you

Is not a life that I want to live.

Fear

You deny yourself
The humanity
That you allow everyone else
And you suffer for it.
You bring cartloads
Of baggage that you swear you are over
But their weight drags you down
Into the deepest part of yourself.
It is murky there
And it smells like sadness.
It is where your childhood lies.
In a dreary room
Painted purple
With dated wallpaper border
And the smell of fear.
You are not alone in this life
As you thought you were as child.
So many of us have walked along
The cold pavement of our former selves
Only to find ourselves
Among friends.

Motherhood

Disbelief

I would tell you that you are beautiful
But you wouldn't believe me.
I would tell you that you are the perfect mom,
But you'd scoff.
I would tell you that your body
Is fit
For the gods,
But you would frown and think about dieting.
I would tell you that you are amazing
And you'd blush
In disbelief.
I would tell you that you need to know
These things
To make beauty out of your life
And you would know that I speak
The truth
And still put yourself
Last.

Love is Feeling

Love does not make everything
Better.
A mother loves her child
Unquestionably.
It doesn't make her a
Good mother.
It makes her human.
Being a good mother
Requires that we know
Ourselves
So that we don't unwittingly
Fall into old patterns of love
That were poisonous.
Being a good mother
Means seeing yourself
Clearly
And behaving in accordance
With your values.
Love doesn't conquer all
For mothers.
Love doesn't conquer all for anyone.
Love is a feeling.

Motherhood is therefore
A series of actions
That allow
A young life to flourish
Amid the insanity
Of this world.

Universal Folds

Mama,
You are built of steel
And bone
Covered in soft
Warm flesh
That holds
Thousands
Of lives
In its folds.
You are the universe
Made mortal
Dripping with life.
There are no chains
That can contain
You
Your power is miraculous
And terrifying
You are the world
Not just to the human
You have birthed
But to everyone
Who dares
Cross your path.

Not Without You

Mama.
You are worth it.
You are not lost
But found.
You are beautiful.
You are enough.
You are elegant.
You are kind.
You are brave.
You are strength.
You are a promise for the future.
You are seen.
You are heard.
You are life.
The world wouldn't be the same
Without you.

Sit in the Fire

You can heal Mama.
Just like your battered and bruised body
After birth
You can heal.
You can know yourself
Again.
You can reclaim your life,
Your body,
Your soul,
From the vastness
Of uncertainty.
Of avoidance.
You can agree
To take care of yourself
Again.
You can commit to finding joy.
You can love what you once loved
Or cast it off
For something new.
You can sit in the fire
Of your life
And not feel defeated.

You can create the life you want.
You can have the happiness
That you seek.
You can be something in addition
To being someone's
Everything.
You can sing.
You can dance.
You can live.

<u>My Table</u>

Come and sit
At my table
Mama.
Tell me your truth.
Your truth is everything.
You are everything.

Never Alone

If motherhood has brought
You darkness,
You are not alone.
If you have lost
Important pieces
Of yourself
To motherhood,
You are not alone.
If you are still finding
Yourself
As a mother,
You are not alone.
If most mornings,
You wake up
And fear that you can't
Do it all again,
You are not alone.
If you feel like you are failing,
You are not alone.
If you are the most
Powerful force
In the universe
And cannot yet see that clearly,
You are not alone.

You Don't Have to Say It's Worth It

You don't have to exclusively
Breastfeed.
You don't have to play all the
Enriching games.
You don't have to puree your own
Baby food.
You don't have to send
Love notes
In lunches.
You don't have to shuttle
Your kid to 10 different
Activities.
You don't have to go
To playdates.
You don't have to
Enjoy every minute.
You don't have to be perfect.
You don't have to know
What you are doing.
You don't have to find
Fulfillment
In being a mother.
You don't have to want

Or have
More children.
You don't have to live up
To ideals
About what a good mother is.
You don't have to
Sacrifice yourself
Or your sanity.
You don't have to say
That it's all worth it.
You don't have to have a clean house.
You don't have to see your kid's behaviour
As a reflection of your parenting.
You don't have to have
The perfect child.
You don't have to be married
Or partnered.
You don't have to put everyone's needs
Before your own.
You don't have to
Do everything.
This is your life.
Decide how you want to
Live it.

"Mummy"

I am not going to eviscerate
Myself
With the idea
That one day
One day
I might hate myself
Because of how much
I miss
Her calling me
Mummy.

Altered

Mama.
Your life isn't
Over.
I promise.
Yes, you have
Died.
You are altered.
You are
Different.
But it is in this
Death
That you are
Reborn.

Betrayal

Pretending to be
Perfect
Is the ultimate
Betrayal
Of other
Mothers.

A Prayer for New Mothers

You think you'll never sweep
The floor again,
That your breasts will never be
Something other
Then that which trickle
Sickly sweet milk down
Your newly
Misshapen belly.
You'll think that
Life is over
And it is
At least as you knew it.
What you soon discover
Is a new life.
Not just the one
Squiggling upon your lap
But one that will open
The oceans
Of your heart
And leave you gasping tears
Of joy and fear
Forever into
The future.

Kitchen Witch

You never imagined
That you'd be some
Kind
Of second-rate
Kitchen witch.
Degrees never framed.
Living an
Unimaginable
Life.
And maybe the worst
Part
Is that you and your
Dishpan hands
Wouldn't be anywhere
Else.

<u>Crumpled Dreams</u>

There is no weakness
In motherhood.
Only crumpled
Dreams
And battered
Warriors.

Tempering

I get weak-kneed
Blurry
And red
Eyed
Trying to be
Everything
To everyone.
My feelings
Surface
Raw and bloodied
Like cold beef
Tempering
On the counter.
And I realize
That I cannot be
Enslaved
By the fear
Of rejection
When all I want to be
Is desperately
Me.

Tiny Hands

I never thought
That I would be
The centre of another's
Comfort.
Realizing that I can
Soothe
With my body
Is second
Only
To coming to terms
With the fact
That it also built
The tiny hands
That now hold my face
With love.

A Warning

Whispers
Of decadent
Silence
Is a longing that
Mothers
Uniquely feel.
Silence may be
Deadly
But mothers
Are brave
Beyond measure.
Don't fuck with us.
I warn you.

<u>Sorry</u>

I'm sorry
That no one has ever
Really
Listened
To you
In that way
Where it is abundantly
Clear
That you are being
Understood.
I'm sorry
That you
Have to do the work
Of three men
And it still
Isn't good enough.
I'm sorry
That you
Have to explain
What life is like
Inside your
Body

To those
Who don't deserve
To know.

A Mother's Day Prayer

May all mothers know
Their true worth.
May all of us support
Each other.
May all of us recognize
That there is no perfect
Way to be a mother.
May all mothers know
That motherhood is not
A competition.
May all mothers know
That you don't have to
Love motherhood
To be a good mother.
May all mothers
Prioritize themselves
And know
That the power
Of the universe
Lies inside
Their hearts.

Intersection

After you are torn
Open
By something that
Feels
Like love and fear
But is called birth,
You are asked to
Rebuild yourself
One fragile
Cell
At a time.
Good luck
Finding the
Intersection
Of who you are
And who you were
While keeping
Everyone
Alive.

Workhorse

You are so much more
Thank a clean house
And a small waist
A workhorse
That is whipped
Toward it's untimely
Death.
Remember how
You were made
To be everything?
The star of the show
The top of your class
The life of the party.
Drudgery does not
Look
Good on you
Nor does the belief
That this is your lot
In life.
Smell the air
Touch your skin
Live like you matter
Mama.

Cracked Up

The relentlessness
Of motherhood
Cracks me up
Literally cracks my teeth
Fills me with tension
And sheer exhaustion
That only parents
And those who work the
Graveyard shift too long
Really know
Intimately
Moms are angry
And want the grinding work
To cease
But instead
We grind our bones
And snort life into ourselves
So that we can face
Another
Tomorrow.

Reservoir

Mercifully,
I'm sitting alone
The chatter of my
Five-year-old
Stalled
Momentarily
So I can grasp
At breaths
And try to claw the
Tired
Out of my eyes.
All while
Suppressing
Fears of the future
Which is unknown,
Unstable,
And increasingly
Asking me to dig
Deeper into the
Reservoir of myself
To see if I have
Anything
Left.

Blood, Sweat, & Tears

It's no wonder
That those who hold
Up
The universe
Can barely hold up
Their heads.
Now is the time
To abandon
The rules
That were written
By privileged men
In quiet studies
Who didn't know the
Stench
Of baby shit
Mixed with their own
Blood
Sweat
And tears.

Carrion Confession

There are days
That I'd like to cut
Out
My tongue
For being so salty.
There are days
When "Mummy"
Is the worst
Sound
In the world.
There are days
When I want
To rip my skin
Off
And feed it to the
Birds
Like some kind
Of carrion
Confession.

Embodying the Beast

When I became a mother
It stole my soul
My time
My mind.
I had to beg for them back.
I had to convince
Myself that I could do
The job of a lifetime.
I had to accept the title
Mother.
I had to eat my
Ignorance.
I had to step up
And embody
The beast.

Grim Reaper

It's strange to be
A mother
Afraid of babies
Watching the
Grim Reaper
Touch your face
And want you to
Love Every Minute.
If motherhood
Isn't yours
It belongs to
Fear
And fear has
No place
In the universe
That is you.

<u>Harlot</u>

So you didn't love
Your baby
Like some kind of
Disney villain
Or biblical harlot
Your heart didn't ooze
With love
And only your eyes
And pussy
Cried silent tears
For a life
Lost
And a life
Gained.

I Am Home

I am no Mama Bear
Stereotype
No adrenaline-fuelled
Heroine
Lifting a car
Off of her child.
I am the soft and warm
Place
My daughter calls
Home
And I never need to
Prove that
To anyone but her.

Liquid Love

Mama,
In the space
Between servitude
And avoidance
Your freedom
Lies.
In stolen moments
Of hot breath
And liquid love
You'll find your
Refuge.
There are no
Planes
Or trains
That can take you
Instead, you must
Insist that you
Are worth
The time and the
Effort
That you give to
Everyone else.

There Will Be Blood

The things that I wish I knew:
There will be blood.
There will be fear.
There will be an unrecognizable
Face and body.
There will be a stranger that you
Must dedicate your life to.
There will be anger, resentment,
And regret.
Amidst all of that, there will be a spark
Of love.

Awakening

Motherhood is a series of small and large deaths.
The death of self.
The birth of power.
Motherhood will continually rip the rug from under you.
Cut you off at the knees.
You will be disabled.
You will be made to fear for your life and the lives of others.
You will gasp for breath through tears, both happy and sad.
You will know what it is to beg.
You will feel lost in the deep dark wood.
And slowly, so slowly, you will find rebirth.
You will slowly awaken again.
Like a bear getting droplets of melting ice on her fur in springtime.
You will look around one day and say, "Omg. I'm living again."
I have rediscovered life.
This happened to me in the woods yesterday.
A little awakening.

A tiny rebirth.

There she was.

Walking in the woods in front of me.

Doing one of my all-time favourite activities - walking in the woods in fall.

What was dormant or altered for years, sprang to life in me.

Crisp leaves.

Colourful mushrooms.

Life and death surrounding me.

As it has been and forever shall be now that I am a mother.

Faint of Heart

I am not the bravest or the kindest mom.
I am not the kind of mom who longs to be motherly.
I am not the kind of woman who always chooses to be
a mom.
I am not the worst mom or the best mom.
I am not the mom I had or the mom I thought I'd be.
I am always surprising myself as a mom.
Surprised by my ability to love and learn.
Surprised by my ability to make things work, to come
up with explanations for the world's more inane and
inspiring things.
Surprised that I love bugs as much as my daughter
does.
Surprised that I can draw on the strength of those
who love me to fuel my motherhood.
Motherhood is not for the faint of heart.
Or for the weak.
Weak is what motherhood makes you.
Weak in the knees.
Weak from the weeping of your heart.
Mothers have to steel ourselves in the face of our
children's sadness.

Their fear.

Their reluctance to go on alone or their haste to put distance between themselves and your arms.

Motherhood will break you.

I guarantee you that.

And that breaking will make you stronger like when bones forge a forever bond after shattering to dust inside you.

Motherhood is a path like no other.

One of destruction and despair.

One of magic, wonder, and true miracles.

Motherhood teaches you the good and the bad.

And it makes you beg and pray for the solace of knowing that you are doing it okay.

Pure Love

That face.
Your face.
Painted on my heart.
Guiding the light inside me.
Your face.
That face.
Wanting all of me
Completely.
Always finding your home
In me.
Mummy.
That face.
Your precious face.
Granting me the privilege
Of purpose.
Of satisfaction.
Of a true taste of love.
A kind of love that turns you
Inside out
And doesn't let you
Rest.
Doesn't let you

Forget who you are
Despite being lost in
Being Mummy.
A kind of love
That nothing can replicate.
Nothing can compare to.
Nothing can crumble.
Not even shifting tectonic plates
Or the total blackout of the sun.
That face.
That face.
Everything about it
Says to me,
Perfection.
Possibility.
Purpose.
Pure love.
Pure, pure love
From the deepest well
Of my being.

The Wrong Monster

Do you want to know why you are angry?
Because you are tired Mama.
Tired of details.
And planning.
And trying to make room in a life where things just
won't fit.
Oh, the resentment is real.
You think about all the time you used to have.
And squandered.
Thinking that you were busy.
You didn't realize that what you were feeling
Was a life that was your own.
Things don't often work out
The way women want them to.
We make choices that pile
Duty at our feet.
We get swallowed up by others.
Their wants and needs
And priorities.
We get tired.
And tired so often turns to anger.
We don't know what to do with how we feel

And the only way we've been taught to externalize is
to make it someone else's fault.
But we blame the wrong monster.
We think it's because of him, or her, or this or that,
But we don't realize
That we're caught in a trap.
We been set up since birth.
Stamped on every girl's forehead
It says,
At your service.
That's how we find our value.
And that's how we tap into our rage.
What isn't fair is that we are often too tired to fight
The real enemy
Which has worked its way into our soul
And told us that we are only good enough
If...

<u>Ghost Self</u>

I am the ghost of my former self.
Long lost in memories of an identity that doesn't
seem like it ever even mattered.
Not ever.
Someone before
Mother.
Someone before
This swirl of expectation
And service.
The stranglehold of
Being everything for
Another.
Circling like a vulture around middle age and landing
in a place that feels unfamiliar,
Equally drawn toward birth
And death.
This is a place where everything
That has always been
Familiar
Seems foreign
And strange.
What's your purpose?

Who have you always been?
Are you going to be lost
Between your
Selves
Forever,
Or struggle to find
A new identity
Inside
The abyss
Of never having really
Known yourself?

Mercy

I am going to tell you
Secrets
With a shame-stained
Tongue.
I am going to snap
You awake
Because modern day
Motherhood
Asks for sleepless
Zombies,
Mary Magdalenes
With no room for
Mercy for
Themselves.
You can deny
That you feel
Resentment
And anger
And frustration
About who you are supposed
To be
Since birth

But that doesn't
Serve
Anyone
Except those
Who would prefer
That you shut up
And stayed
In your
Place.

Multiplication

There are little white pills to keep you stable
Fried food to keep you sane.
You long for someone who isn't you
To come back and inhabit
Your soul.
You pretend that things were better then,
In a time filled with the uncertainty of being
Even though life is so much clearer now.
You have all this desperate purpose
And life is triply worth living
But you long for silence
And time to work on the frivolous stuff you love.
You want to lay in the spring sun
Stretched out on the floor
Like a cat
And lap milk from an endless
Bucket of selfishness
Like the kind that you squandered
Before you knew what it was like
To be twinned,
And multiplied,
By love.

A Mother's Labour

I abhor admonitions to enjoy.
I will not.
I will only enjoy on my terms.
Based on my measures of success.
Of sanity.
I will not be placated
By "messy home, full heart"
Bullshit.
How about:
Messy home,
Scattered mind,
Fractured heart,
Scorching nerves.
That rings truer.
It makes me feel seen.
Heard.
Cared about.
Like my labour,
The sheer staggering
Enormity
Of a mother's labour
Then actually takes its place
In the centre of the fucking universe.

My Truth

My truth feels wrong and shameful.
It is about a life
That was ruined.
That I can't let go of.
Is it possible to love something
And also mourn what it took from you?
Motherhood robbed me of me
And yet I'm supposed to love it.
It pulled the ground from under my feet
And left me dazed
To pick up the shards of my former self.
I'm still broken
And resentful.
Petulant
Like a child.
I don't blame my child
For taking what was mine,
A life I loved and nurtured
With the kind of care
You bestow on baby birds
That have fallen from the nest.
I guess I still blame myself
For not knowing
What was to come.

Meatsuits

What the World Needs

Mama,
You are utter perfection.
The folds of your soft skin.
The lines on your beautiful face.
You radiate truth and love.
You glow with a fire that ignites
Your eyes.
You are dreams
And whispers.
You are what the world needs
More of.

All I Want/Precious Garbage

All I want
Is space to
Breathe,
For someone to tell me
It will all be okay.
Faith in my
Inability
To be caged and tamed
And a celebration
That involves
Eating the skin
I grow out of
And shed
Like so much
Precious garbage.

Fading Paper

You are not
Your face
Or your milk-sucked
Tits.
You are not your partner's
Prize
Or your baby's
Chew toy.
You are not
Your job
Or a title
Or a piece of fading paper
Hung up in a room
That no one
Goes into.
You are not your past
And your fragile
Dreams
Of frivolous things.
You are a vast collection
Of strength
And sadness

And struggle
That jumbles
Into something that
Resembles
A shaky kind
Of grace.

Beautiful Wild

All the ways
You think that you are
Imperfect.
All the vile ways
You tell yourself
You are not enough.
All the energy you expend
Hating your body
The quality of your skin
The turn of your nose
The angle of your eyes.
My prayer
Is that you go gently
With yourself
Now and into the future
Because your beautiful wildness
Deserves to be nurtured
Like the tiniest baby
So it can grow
Into what you were
Always meant to be.

Inside Out

You think perfection is the answer
And you are wrong.
You think people liking you is the answer
And you are wrong.
You think turning yourself
Inside out
For acceptance
Is the answer
And you are wrong.
You think that coming more into
Being
Fully who you are
Will make them
Love you
And you are wrong.
You think the answer
Lies in more
Different
Better
New
And you are
Wrong.

Glory

If I believed that
Being thinner
Would make you happy,
I would tell you
To do that.
If I thought
Perfection
Was the key
I would advise it
If I imagined that you could
Will yourself into love,
I would command it.
But the only thing
That will free you
Is you.
The hardest thing
That you will ever do
Is accept yourself.
That acceptance
Is the basis of your
Glory
Your success.
Your everything.

Curves

The only way
That you could be
More perfect
Is if you
Wholeheartedly
Accepted
The subtle and beautiful
Ways
Your body curves
And dances
Under the fingertips
Of someone
You love.

Portal

Your body
Has housed life
And a million
Splintered
Pieces of who you are
And want to be.
Memories
And horror stories
Beautiful breaths
And clean fresh air
And wicked sins
That make you feel alive.
Your body
Is neither
A vessel
Nor a portal
But it is what makes
The earth turn
And the rain
Fall.

Delicious

You are allowed
To be what size
You are.
You are allowed to take
Up space.
You are allowed to make
Decisions
About just you.
You are exquisite.
You are delicious.
You, you, you.
You can, My Lovely.
Just do it.
No questions.
No regrets.

Stumbling

Of, but aren't you
Exquisite
In your exhaustion.
The kind
You reserve
For those you love
With a rawness
That you can't taste.
And don't you wish
That everything
Could be the same
And different
As you walk in shoes
That are too big
For you
And make you stumble
Over and over again
To your
Bloody knees.

Juicy

Maybe softness
Is your word
This year
So that you can
Roll it around
Your tongue
In ways that
Touch
The soft folds
Of your skin
And send tingles
Of pulsing
Blood
To every
Juicy
Bit of you.

Wither

The lines on your face
Deserve grace.
I'm not scared.
If you're not.
Let's wither
Into something
Exquisite together,
Shall we?

Fecund

Oh my.
Aren't you soft and
Beautiful
Like some kind of
Spring unfolding
As though your
Your breasts
Don't bud
Anymore
As though your
Fecundity
Has anything to do
With babies.
Your ripeness
Is transfixing
And you can feel it
Regardless of any eyes
To see it.
You know,
You Sultry Bitch.
You know.

I Won't

No
I won't make
Myself smaller
Or more
Palatable
More desirable
For anyone
But me.
I won't
Count calories
I won't
Run till
I puke
I won't berate myself
For chips
And life
And living
On my terms
I don't need
Anyone's
Permission
To be
Me.

Chasms

Here's an ice cream
Scoop
To carve out
My heart.
Here's a blade
To use
To open
And navigate
My veins.
A woman's worth
Is not written
On her body
Unless you go
Searching
In the deep
Chasms
Between her legs
Or buried
Deep
Within
Her soul.

Feisty AF

Naw.
I won't plump my lips.
And add hair there.
I won't comply.
You can't make me.
I'm feisty as fuck
And if you want
Something
From me
You better ask
Cause this shit's
Not
Free.

Thick & Meaty

I'm thick.
Meaty
My breasts are
Rotund.
I'm rippled
And slightly
Puffy
In all the imperfect
Places
And my brain wants
Me to apologize
For taking
Up space.
But I'm not
Embarrassed
About living free
Of the shadow fear
Of my own
Fat.

Hustling

You are beautiful and
Brilliant
And you spend most of
Your time
Lamenting what you
Just ate.
You can see freedom
But are too busy
Hustling
For the love of those
Who don't
Deserve you.
You know you're
Worth it
But spend all of your
Time
Asking others if you
Matter
Thinking the whole
Time
That you're the only
One
Who hates
Herself.

Liquid Honey

There are exquisite
Evenings
That remind me of you
Who you are
Water kisses your
Curves
Like it knows every
Inch of you
Wantingly caressing
You like a lover.
You're awake in your
Life
Not treading water
And the air in your
Lungs
Tastes
Like liquid honey.

Naked & Afraid

There was a time
That I would stand
Naked and afraid
And hope that you
Wouldn't judge me
Too harshly.
There was a time when
I thought that it
Mattered if you cared
Or thought
I was pretty.
That's over now.
As I reach into the
Decades of freedom
That spill out
Before me
Because I know that
Peace doesn't come
By asking for it.

Unfettered

You can hate yourself
Or you can live life on your terms.
You can live in fear
Or you can make
Choices that are
Unfettered by what
People think of you
Or think you should do.
You can own your body
Or you can punish it
And tell yourself
You're garbage
Or you can spend
Your time being
Brilliant
Beautiful
And brave.

Rule the World

Sometimes I feel lumpy
And bumpy
And insanely
Powerful
Like I could crush
You
With my thighs.
Maybe someone
Somewhere
Realized that if we're
Hungry
We're less likely
To rule the world
With our sex.

Ample Tits/Juicy Bits

I'm scared
Of my ample tits
Thighs
Juicy bits.
I'm thick
And all kinds
Of too much
Spilling into
Tomorrow
Because you can't
Keep me bound to
Today
You can't catch me
Know me
Watch me
Enjoy myself
Because you think
That it's unimaginable
Without your scent.
How does it feel
Sweetheart
To be
Obsolete.

<u>Saviour</u>

I'd be sexy
But I'm too busy
Being an intellectual
And trying not to worry
If my face is enough.
I would not age
Gracefully
If I thought
That I had a chance
At denying every wrinkle
And line
That (de)forms
My face.
I want you to know
That no one
Defines you
And when you
Feel lost
Only you
Are your saviour.

Content

I am aging.
Life creeps up
Like tangled ivy
Trying to
Strangle
Out the light.
All I have is what is
Important
Which is not
A lot
But so much more
Than enough.
If the fear that
Looms
Is sadness
Know that sadness
Isn't death
Sadness is the space
Where
Contentment
Takes root.

<u>Holy Grail</u>

I used to think
That a woman's job
Was to please someone
Between
Her knees
And then I realized
That pleasure
Only comes
When the juiciness
On and between
Our thighs
Is not seen
As a Holy Grail
But instead
A place where
Peace and power collide.

Tell Me What You Want

I could tell you
What to do
With your life
Your hair
Your relationship
And act as though
You haven't spent
Your life
Being told
Not to
Trust yourself
Imagine a world
Were instead
I said,
Tell me what
You want
So that I can help you
Get what you
Deserve.

Warm Body

I have known
Perfectly floral-scented
Women
Who do not know
That they should be
More discerning
With their affection.
I have known
Brown-eyed
Men who have
No business
In the hearts and minds
Of perfectly crafted
Brilliant and curvaceous
Queens.
But sometimes
The bridge
Between these souls
Is made up of failure
To feel adequate
And an aching
Need

For a warm body
In the middle
Of the night.

Hot Breath

There is nothing
More beautiful
Than the space
Between hot breaths
Whether breathed
Against the inside
Of your thigh
Or gently
Blown on
The microscopic
Hairs
That cover your
Beautiful face.
You're wrong
To think
That you're not
Beautiful
Because there is
Nothing
More beautiful
Than you.

Gravitational Pull

Some days
You will feel alive
With the buzzing
Of thousands
Of nerve endings
Pressed against the
Surface
Of your skin.
Some days
You will feel heavy
With everything
Pressing you
Down further
Into the earth's
Gravitational pull.
Both states are fine
It's just that you
Judge
One
More than
the other.

<u>Bitter Pills</u>

There are desperate wants
That travel through
Your veins
Asking you
To finally
Let you be enough.
Enough for you.
For him.
For them.
Enough.
You sweat
And starve
And want
Because you think
Deprivation
Will make you feel full.
There is poison
That you feed yourself
And call it medicine.
The only medicine that will
Save you now
Is truth

Swallowed
Like the bitterest
Of pills.

Magnificent Disaster

There is nothing you need to do.
Nothing you need to be.
To be perfect.
You are glorious
In all your stretch-marked beauty.
The lines on your face,
Your supple belly,
Your kind eyes
And generous laugh.
You are everything.
There is nothing that you need to change.
There is nothing wrong with you.
You are brilliant and resourceful and purposeful.
You can rest.
You can stop working on yourself as a project.
You can stop shaming yourself into submission.
Submission is for those who don't know their value,
Who don't keeping showing up
And getting up
Over and over again.
You are devastating in your perseverance.
You are plain in your purpose.

You just want to live your truth.
Your absolute truth.
And that makes you magnificent
Even in disaster.

House of Dreams

What shame is there in having a body
One that has housed dreams
And life
And silent flickers
Of broken memory.
Tender touches
In darkened rooms.
What shame is there
In letting oneself
Go
In the sense
That women are already asked
To sacrifice
So much
In the name of acceptability.
There is no laziness
In womanhood.
There is only toil
That comes
From marching to drums
That we should steal
And burn

And forget the crushing beat of.
There is no shame
In luscious curves
That a world of gluttony
Desires to deprive you of
So that you may show
Your worth
To a king
That you would never
Bow to.

<u>Scars</u>

There are
Gorgeous
Ebbs and flows
To life
That are terrifying
And wonderful.
There is the kind of
Change
That pulls you
Under
And drags you
Mercilessly
Along the ocean
Floor.
Ripped flesh
And oozing wounds.
Your life story
Written in scars.

Monstrous

Cages

Don't worry about babies in cages or
Despots in higher office.
Don't think that there might be any
Connection
In the not-so-vast space
Between us and them.
Don't think that these things happen elsewhere,
Or try to deny that democracy and human rights
Are piles of shit in your country too.
Don't call me tender-hearted,
Or tell me that someone's
Here to steal work that I don't want to do
Or kill me in the name of Allah
When you know as well as I do
That Allah is peace by
Another name.
Don't try to convince me that the criminals
Are anyone other
Than those who would build walls
So that children can die on the backs of their fathers
In the mud.
Don't tell me what to think about

A reality that you can't imagine
For your children
Your country
Your life
That is allowed to happen under the noses of
Those who have everything so
That so many can have
Nothing.

Surprise Party

Weathered breasts
And floundering hopes
We walk decades
As though they
Will never end.
Death hovers
Like a warm
And tragic
Stink
A surprise party
That no one
Wants
Or is prepared for.

Life & Death

The taste of our own humanity
Hits
Bitterly on our
Tongues
As we try to explain
That certain parts
Of our walk
Upon the earth
Will buckle our knees
And invite us
To crumble into ruin
Even thought we are
Merely encountering
The fact
That life and death
Will continually meet,
Always and forever.

Vector of Love

I am a vector
Of love
Not a harbinger of
Disease
Awed by the bravery
Of homemade masks
And the willingness to
Wade into
Merciless waters
To save those who,
Before the dawn of a
New decade,
Presumed they were
Safe
From death's unyielding
Knell.

A Sunday Prayer

We have never been
So alone together.
Eating,
Sitting,
Praying,
Loving,
Fighting,
Chasing away
Collective fears.
If you feel alone
Know that we feel alone.
If you feel scared,
Know that we feel scared.
This collective
Journey
We are on
Only works if we're
All in this
Alone together.

Dirt Cloud

Sometimes the stink
Of sadness
Hangs around me
Like Pig Pen's
Dirt cloud.
No purpose
Or rectification
Just heaviness
Threatening to burst
Out of my eyes
Choked
And cloaked
I want to hide
But my mother always
Taught me
That it was better
To just
Cry.

Slippery

While our feet
Might be bloodied
And our hands
Slippery from holding
Onto the wrong
Kinds of love
We have hearts
Bathed in calm
Because we trust
In the goodness
Of the world.
I won't look away
From horror
Because I know
That there is
Nothing
That cannot be
Overcome
On the other side
Of darkness.

Fortress of Solitude

So you're afraid of
Black bodies
And difference
Only comfortable with
Being surrounded
In museums
And on vacation
But never too close
For comfort.
And in your privileged
Fortress of solitude
You think
That you're not like
Them
Neither the oppressed
Nor the oppressor
But what you are quite
Certain about is that
No one gets killed
That hasn't
That isn't
Wrong.

Arbitrar of Goodness

Oh I see.
You think you get to
Decide
Who matters.
You want to frame the
Conversation like some
Referee
Of life
Some arbitrar
Of goodness
As though your whiteness
Will always protect you
From unjust death
From brutal and bloody
Attacks in the street.
You've bought the lie that
Your skin is impenetrable
While you try to make it so
By saying.
See,
They're not like me.

"True North"

White folks
Don't wanna be
Decentered.
They're used to being
Everyone's Truth North.
Standing in
For silenced lives
Just like the dude
Who tells you that
Your experience didn't happen
That way.
Fuck with their
Privilege
And they'll show you
An underbelly
Of impotent rage
Just a wisp below
The surface
Of their celebration
Of diversity.

Grasping

Living in the confines
Of your fear
Is ugly.
It makes you small
And it makes you grasp
At things
That you know
Have no value.
There seems little
Reason
To reject
The box
The world has put you
In
Except that grasping
Is not living
And fear
Is far from
Truth.

May You Know Peace

May you know peace.
The kind of peace that
Keeps you safe
In the streets
In your housed
While you run.
May your voice
Call for your mama
Only for joy
Only for happiness
Only without fear.
May you walk the earth
Unfettered
Unaccosted by
Hate.
May no one
Die in your name
And may no one die by
The hand
Of those
Who are supposed
To protect
You.

Father

We are taught that
Men
Are not nurturing
But this is a lie
To free them from
Domestic drudgery.
We believe it is the
Anomalous man
Who lavishes love
Upon
His child
The falsity of this
Belief is evidenced
By every man who knows
That to be a Father
Means love,
True partnership,
And the same requisite
Devotion and
Self-sacrifice
That women are so
Routinely
Shamed into.

Mascara-Based Confidence

Some days are for
Accepting what is.
Some days are for
Crying.
Some days are for
Mascara-based
Confidence.
Some days are for
Acknowledging that the
Pit in your stomach
Won't kill you
It's just an early
Warning system
That you are being far too
Hard
On yourself.

Fury

Finger wags
Of fury
And I'm just spent
Crawling around
In the heat
Praying for relief
And knowing that none
Is on the horizon
For mothers
Who don't have answers
To basic questions
And women will
Lose much more than
Everyone thinks
They've gained.
It's like we've
Learned nothing from
All the hate
That ignorance has bred in the vilest
Corners of the highest
Offices.

Say Yes

Sometimes agony
Coils around you
Grasping at your
Breath
Asking you to kneel
Not letting you come
Up
For air
Until you do the thing
That ultimately
Saves you:
Saying yes to yourself
And knowing that the
World still turns
Without your intricate
Machinations.

Arrogant Woman

I'm not afraid of your
Anger
Even though you want
Me to be.
I've never thought
Much of arrogant men,
But give me an
Arrogant woman
And I will show you
The path to freedom
And startling
Naked,
Self-discovery.

Desperation

The nights move
Closer
And I'm afraid
Of first snowfalls
And isolation.
I lived on an island
Once
And lonely
Isn't quite the right
Way
To explain my
Almost crippling
Desperation.

Ghosts

There is fear
And then there is
Tear up
Your insides
Terror.
There are ghosts
That haunt us
That were born in
Our cribs
Who we will always
Run from
If we don't eventually
Invite them
For some talk
And tea.

Pleasing

You can keep
Pretending
That you are kind
By nature
And not just
Begging
To be liked.
You can keep compromising
Who you are
For being pleasing
Or you can decide
That respecting
Yourself
And what you need
Is the only way
To really
Live.

New Castles

As I negotiate
The space
Where
I am not quite your
Mother yet
But you also
Don't want to
Fuck me
I'm burning wet with
Desire
To be myself
And don't care
Where I fit
In your schema
Because I am busy
Building
New castles
Erecting new ceilings
That you can't even find
Let alone
Break.

Hercules

Yesterday
I saw you riding
Your bike
And I thought,
Thank god
You're still alive
But then
As you passed
And I looked
Closer
At your sunken
Eyes
Partially covered
By a ratty hat
I realized
No,
You are still dead
And you are not
Coming back
To walk the earth
Half-clad
And herculean.

Worry Dolls

Tell the truth
They say,
But wait,
Not your truth
The truth about
How schoolboys
Harass you
And you never feel
Safe
How the worry dolls
Your bought in Mexico
Aren't quite doing the
Trick
And how much you pray
That one day
You will find
The courage
To say the words
That are true
To you.

Silence

There are men
Who will drag you
To the darkest
Depths
Because they are weak
But surround themselves
With the pretense
Of power.
There are men
Who will lie to
Your face
And then tell you to
Thank them
We can let them into our
Homes
Or in public office
But they will always
Destroy you
If we honour
The horror
Of their crimes
With our silence.

Gods & Monsters

There are gods
And monsters
That roam
This earth.
Neither are
Particularly benevolent
But there is a base
Monster
Who trades
In appearance
And pussies
And then there
Are gods
Who might
Smite you
But at least they know
That there is a
Difference
Between good
And evil.

A Community Prayer

Connection
Underneath dull
Grey skies
Is crucial
For the survival
Of the species.
We act like
Human resilience
Is a thing of
The past
A 1918
Mystery
When we live
In times of death
And ring in
A new year
Full of hope
And something bigger
Something stronger
Than ourselves.

Apathy

The cusp
Of the new year
Hangs
Like hope
On the masked faces
Of the masses.
We pretend
That there will be
Difference
Because hope
Allows for all manner
Of delusion
And for the suspension
Of dim reality.
Don't fret
Over sameness
As only apathy
Kills.

Lessons

I close
My eyes
And kiss
The blood-encrusted
Lips of the past year
With a tear
Not because
I will miss it
But because of what it gave me.
There are lessons
You think you'll
Never get to learn
Until
The fate of the world
Hangs sharply
In the balance.

Hate

We thought
We had made
Progress
Didn't we?
So sure that our
Inhumanity
Was a thing of the
Past.
And then.
And then.
A fury was unleashed
By an orange man
In an expensive suit
And we watched
Dumbfounded
As though hate
Had taken
A forever
Holiday.

Limits

Did he groom me?
I still don't know
Delusional and young
Thinking that I had
A modicum of control
Feeling special
Mature
Wanted
Pretending to know
My limits
While barreling
Headfirst into
His alternate reality
Where we were friends
Innocent enough
It seemed.

Bullies

Sometimes my heart
Feels
Slippery
Like I can't
Get a hold of it
Properly.
It feels squeezed
And hard
In my chest
Cutting off my
Ability
To see and hear
The ones who care
And instead
Showing the faces
Of long ago
Bullies
Who put marks
On my heart
In the first place
And then they said
That they
Were just
Joking.

Tomorrow

It is often easier to situate your struggles in the past.
As though you have overcome them,
By some superhuman moral feat.
It is hard to say,
I struggle.
I am struggling.
I am bobbing on the surface of life in the way that
seaweed does,
Not sure of its final destination.
I struggle.
You struggle.
We have days that turn into nights of terror and angst.
Of discomfort and pain.
When we softly coo to ourselves,
Biting our pillow
Tomorrow is a new day,
Tomorrow will be better.

Sirens

There is a place where pain comes from
That is deep and searing
And seductive
Trying to drag you under
With siren calls
That are deliciously
Loud
And unnerving.
You can sit
And wait to go
Under
Or you can accept
That you want
To be a siren
Luring men
To their death
Because you know
How powerful
You are.

Miracles

I wish I could tell you
That it will
All
Be okay.
But I don't know.
It is.
And then it isn't.
To think that you
Have control
Is a lie that we
Tell ourselves
To make it through.
You don't
Own life
No matter how many
Seize the day
Quotes
You read
You're not in control.
People die
And then loss
Becomes

Real again.
Babies are born
To prove that
Miracles
Happen
Every day.
To know that
We're not in charge
Is less hopeless
Than it is real.
If life becomes
Less solid
Then we
Just might
Make it through.

The Void

There are sicknesses
That cannot be healed
And hearts that cannot
Be unbroken.
There are ways
That the moon
Passes over us
That leave us
Wanton
And stripped bare.
There are days that wind
Endlessly
Into nothingness
And we have to make
Sense
Of the emptiness,
The void.
We have to befriend
Ourselves
And anyone
Whose heart
Burns

For others.
Otherwise
We are alone
With nothing.
For nothing.

Eviscerated

There are many ways
That women
Are sliced up,
Eviscerated
By the world.
We are taught
The ways of hate
For ourselves,
Other women,
Our bodies,
And are convinced that
We cannot
Trust our minds.
Women are stripped
Of everything
Over and over
And yet we survive.
You can take
Everything from us
And we will still
Stand.
You can ruin us

And call us names
Grab us by our
Pussies
And we are still strong.
Stronger
Than you want us
To be.
And braver
Than you
Bargained for.

Magic

Wet

I want to lay
In the hot sun
until
I am wet
With my own
Sweat.
I want to feel
Heat in every
One
Of my pores.
I want to open up
Like a ripe
Coconut
With tender fruit
And salty juice.
I want to bathe
In peace
With myself.
All of myself.

Love

Sometimes smelling
Soft grass
Warmed by the sun
And breathing
Rhythmically
Against
The sound of crickets
Enshrouded
In rows
Of waist-high
Corn
Makes life full of hope
And my heart full
Of what can
Only
Be called
Love.

<u>Set Free</u>

I want to
Pour my heart out
On a plate
To be
Lapped up
By the world.
I want to
Know that I lived
For something
And that maybe
Just maybe
I lived
For everything.
I want to
Set free
The thing
Clawing at my insides
To be released.
I want to live
So close
To the edge
That my eyelashes

Get singed
By fate.
I want to
See my dreams
Come true
Before it's too late
To see what I am
Capable of.
I want to
Be free
In the sense
That life
Is all meaning
And less
Meant to be.

Pause

All I want
Is for your
Anger
Not to eat you
Alive
For your shame
Not to
Break you
And for your
Power
To rise up
And be born
Into something
That gives
The world
Pause.

Death Knell

There are disappointments
That will appear
To be the death
Knell
Of your dreams
But they are simply
Obstacles
In the confrontation
With the truth
Of yourself
That,
Like rings of fire,
Will burn off
Your flesh
That you no longer
Need
And heal into
Scars
That will become
Your saviours.

Afloat

You feel
Useless and alone.
Like all the choices
You've made
Are insubstantial
And for naught.
Like the rivers
Of tears
You've cried
Are meaningless
Stains
On your cheeks
And heart.
But the one thing
You cannot stamp out
Is your hope.
Hope that keeps you
Alive and afloat
And always ready
To try again.
Just one more time.
Just one more time.

Passion

There is a gorgeous week
Stretched out before you like a
Promise.
There are choices
To make
And kindness to bestow.
If life is simply
Acted out
As a series of chores,
We will be dead
With a to-do list
Still on our phone.
Living life
Means more than checking off
Boxes
And doing everything right.
Life is also about purpose
And passion;
Chances taken
And hearts
Broken
And mended.

Heart Inscription

There are friends
And then there are people who
Have etched themselves
Onto your heart.
Have stood beside you
When everyone else
Looked away.
Act like your dreams
Are their dreams.
Sit beside you
When your world
Crumbles
And your soul
Aches.
There are friends
And then there are these people
Sent to you
So that you can
Brave
The world
And yourself.

Glittering Robes

May today bring you
A year of soft kisses,
Warmth that burns
Brightly
From the depths of you.
Kindness like you have
Never known.
May you be wrapped
In glittering robes
Of devotion
And treated like
The angel on
Earth
That you are.

Galloping Beast

I know the thing
That scares you
The galloping beast
In your breast.
To know that you can
Tear down walls
And rebuild them
With your bare and
bloodied hands.
You know that
What you want
Is worth
The price
Of anything
That has ever
Touched
Your hungry lips.

Little Lamb

Tomorrow is coming.
Please treat yourself
Like a little lamb
Lost in the rain.
Soaked fleece.
Full of fear.
Needing comfort.
By extending
Gentleness
To yourself
You change the world.
You break cycles.
You build bridges
Between yourself
And the steady
Beat
Of your formidable
Heart.

Plastic

Just when you think
You will be lost
Forever
Like some kind of
Plastic bag
In the wind.
Tattered and torn
Dirty and useless,
You find yourself
Anew
Almost unrecognizable
In sheer strength
And purpose
That tastes
Like freedom
And makes you
So glad
That you lived.

Spit & Blood

Sometimes your life
Blows up
And you patch it up
With spit
And blood
Futile hope
And tears.
And when you stand
Shakily
In the presence
Of the masterpiece
That is your
Survival
You know that there
Are paths
That you have to take
To live.

<u>Heartbeat</u>

Sometimes your heart
Beats
And your skin crawls
And if you are quiet,
Oh so quiet,
You'll hear your heart
Beat
In unison
With the world
And realize
That it's a good day
To live.

Wet Dirt

And I went out
Into the world
And I tried
To be love
To breathe love
Huffing it
Like a fix of wet dirt
And unfurling leaves
Would calm the tension
In my body
And soul.
Next I'm going to roll
Around
In the ecstasy
Of life
And bring you back
A souvenir.

<u>Precipice</u>

Standing on the
Precipice
All dangling
Flesh
And discarded
Dreams
May we watch
The fall of
Greatness
Give birth
To a better
Tomorrow.

Exquisite Bitch

You ooze love
You exquisite bitch.
I want
To taste
You
But you are already
Familiar
To my tongue.
I love you.
You are not grotesque.
You are everything.
I will fight you
You stubborn
Beautiful
Bitch.

Guts & Glory

I've never been the
Kind of girl
Who would be
Afraid
To eat your heart
Out
With a spoon.
I pride myself
On the kind of
Guts and glory
That men
Cannot stomach.
Don't fear me
For my genius
Just know your
Place
In a hierarchy
That meets
The needs
Of women
And leaves
You wanting.

Resuscitation

If you need me
To resuscitate
The woman you once
Were
I will breathe
My breath
Into your lungs
Until you live again.
If you want magic
I will become the
Circus
So that you know that you are what Life
Is worth living for.
If you need to be reminded that you are everything
We hoped you could be
And more
I will fall to my
Knees
And beg you to see
The worth
That oozes from your every
Pore.

Privilege

You can stand
On the
Edge
Of never enough
Or you can stand
Boldly in your truth.
You can spit the words
Like flames
From anger and outrage
That you are not
Seen
Or you can demand
To be seen.
No one but you
Gets to decide
What you deserve
And if they try to
Deny you
They don't get the
Privilege
THAT IS YOU.

Habitation

If there is a universe
In which I deserve
Your love
May I inhabit it forever.
If there is a space in
Your heart
To allow me to rest
Like a feeble
Helpless
Infant,
May I forever know how
To unlock it.
If there is a way that
I can cut out my heart
So that you may see
The tattoo of you
Staring back,
May I find it
So that the depth of
My love and devotion
Is obvious
And totally obscene.

Offering

I guess
I've realized
That life
Is about ripping
Your heart
Out
Over and over
So that it can keep
Beating
Loving
Living
Feeling.

Heaven on Earth

Some days
Are filled
With bakeries
That smell like
Actual heaven
And women at farm stands
Who guide you
With their gentle
Voices
To see big-footed
Ducks hiding in a hot field.
Some days
You hike up
Mountains
And remember
That there is
Everything
To live for.

Tragic Wonder

I believe in love
And tragic wonder.
I believe in karmic
Fields
Of devastation.
I believe in not
Knowing
Why your dreams are
Filled
With hatred
And blind rage
With orgasmic
Chasers.
I believe that you
Know the truth
And you'll bite off
Your tongue to tell it.

Scavenging

Declaration of
Identity
Are both the most
Powerful
And powerless
Things we can do.
We give ourselves
To others
On a half-devoured
Platter
Apologizing for being the messy
Scavenged
Piecemeal somethings
That we are
But knowing
That without
Our voice
And our truth
Another cannot
Be born
Into full
Intelligibility.

The Power of Love

I will never
Stop believing
In the power of love.
Cynics say that it's
Not enough
And critics say
That it breeds
Complacency
But I know
That love is the only
Thing
That has the power to
Make your groan
Make your grow
And make you gallop
Toward a more
Extraordinary
Tomorrow.

Unmoored

Unmoored
In stillness
Feet just brushing
The ground
Going to that place
Where I am afraid
Of myself
And quietly
Contemplating
What ifs.
Dark weather
And dreary
Thoughts
Try to suppress
The light
Of one thousand
Suns inside me.
Come at me darkness.
I'll eat you up.

Transcendence

Maybe death is just
Life
Reborn anew
In a strange amalgam
Of meat,
And blood,
And bone.
Maybe touching
Death
Is a miracle
Given to us
So that we
Can pave
The way
For less
Bitter endings.

Yawning Ache

Tell them
You love them
Over and over
And over
Until
Your voice
Cracks and departs
Your body.
Keep them
Safe
By holding them
In your heart
And allow
That yawning ache
To lead you
Back into
Their arms.

Sunspot

There is a sun
Spot
On my heart
That whispers
Keep going.
She's always
There
Under the clouds
Pulsing
To the drumbeat
Of my heart.
She trusts
Me more
Than I trust
Myself
And each day
She wakes
And calls me
To be
More of what
I am meant
To be.

Speak the Truth

When women do
What we don't
Want them
To do
We shame them
We do this
Because we know
The force
Of being called
Out
For simply
Pushing the breath
From our throats
And gently
But defiantly
Speaking
The truth.

Droplets

Some days
I want to while
Away
In a little
Cabin
Where no one
Goes.
Some days
I want solitude
To rain down
On me
In heavy
Wet
Droplets.
Some days
I want to
Preach
To choirs
Of angels
About what
Mothers
And women
Really deserve.

An Alarm Clock for the Soul

Sometimes life is a beautiful disaster.
Messy and painful.
Fraught and fearful.
And in your heart you know – no, you trust – that the mess is
meant for you to sit in.
Be exhausted by.
Like a nightmare you wake up from,
So completely and thoroughly relieved
That every horrible thing you can imagine
Isn't really true.
Sometimes life calls you with butterflies
And makes you snap awake
From a dream state that you didn't even know you got
comfortable in.
Sometimes all the pain in the world
Is a message.
An alarm clock for the soul
That tells you to wake the fuck up
And do what you were meant for.

Reclamation

My aunt gave me my word.
Bestowed it like a gift.
Reclamation.
My life.
My time.
My identity.
My world.
When chaos come knocking, we are never prepared.
We think we are.
But we ain't seen nothing yet.
When your world turns to dust, a broom won't cut it.
It takes some heavy lifting.
It takes some trust and vulnerability.
It takes some investment in joy.
So I have to reclaim.
Take what's mine.
In a world that tells you that you have to give
everything.
Every piece of you you are told isn't yours.
You have to give yourself away to be loved.
To be meaningful.
To be a mother.

No one tells you what you deserve or reminds you who you really are.

Well I'm here to tell you - you are worthy of reclamation.

You are worthy of space, needs, wants, desires, preferences, time.

Take it.

Take it back.

And hold onto it like nothing else matters.

Because it doesn't.

Enough

I want to breathe in
The seething fire of purpose
And feel it burn my lungs.
I want to know that just by being
That I am truly enough.
I want to hear the words
I love you
And have them transport me
Back to solid ground.
I want to feel the swirls
Inside my head
Without fear
That I am
Being erased.
I want calm to settle
Like dust on my soul
So that
The world and I
Can be friends
Once again.

Bleeding Out

And then the sun comes out.
You thought it never
Would
Cause your flesh was
On the floor
And you were bleeding out.
But there it is.
In the sky.
Like it never left.
Like it was only behind
The clouds of your
Mind.
The sun dries
My tears.
Repairs my wounds.
Dries up
My rotten bits
And gently brushes
My face.
We can live
Or we can die.
We can accept help

Or we can wallow in
Misery.
Your struggle is
Never
Yours alone.
Let's walk
In the sun
Together.
Let's push through fear
In each other's
Arms.
Let's tell each other
That it will be okay.
And let's make sure
That tomorrow exists
For all of us.

Introduction

I have love
Emblazoned
On my heart
And raw,
Rickety
Resilience
Built into my bones
Which were
Themselves
Built in my mother's
Womb.
I am a tried
And true
Testament
Of what womanhood means
That is,
When life emits
From
You
And takes you to a
Place beyond
Yourself

Introducing you to a
Woman
You never
Knew.

About the Author

Jackie Schoemaker Holmes, PhD is a woman, mom, Sociologist, teacher, and entrepreneur who lives life on her own terms and has been encouraging other women and moms to do that same since she birthed her daughter and lost her mind. She lives in Ontario, Canada with the best partner, kid, and cat and very close to the small town of her birth where her parents still reside in the same red brick bungalow of her youth.

Strident cat mom, feminist, and hopeless optimist, Jackie

now channels her passion and expertise in empowerment into helping women and moms who like her, negotiate contemporary womanhood and motherhood in a world that prefers us to be both convenient and quiet.

Disrupting motherhood is her borderline obsession and she wants to invite you along for the ride by asking you, too, to be a problem for mediocre white men and to blow up societal expectations that seek to strangle our truth and our humanity.

Discover more about Jackie Schoemaker Holmes
and her empowerment work.

Eating Her Young
www.facebook.com/eatingheryoung

Empowerment For Resilience
empowermentforresilience.com

For appearances and media requests, contact
jackie@empowermentforresilience.com

Made in United States
North Haven, CT
07 December 2021

12016593R00136